Children's Authors

Marc Brown

Mae Woods
ABDO Publishing Company

visit us at
www.abdopub.com

Published by ABDO Publishing Company, 4940 Viking Drive, Suite 622, Edina, Minnesota 55435. Copyright © 2001 Abdo Consulting Group, Inc., P.O. Box 398166, Minneapolis, Minnesota 55439 USA. International copyrights reserved in all countries. No part of this book may be reproduced in any form without written permission from the publisher.

Printed in the United States.

Photos: Robert Muller, Cleveland Institute of Art (pages 5, 9); Corbis (pages 11, 17, 21); Marc Brown Studios (cover, page 13); John L. Scott, Scott Historical Photos (page 7)
Editors: Bob Italia, Tamara L. Britton, Kate A. Furlong, Christine Fournier
Art Direction: Neil Klinepier

Library of Congress Cataloging-in-Publication Data

Woods, Mae.
  Marc Brown / Mae Woods.
      p. cm. -- (Children's authors)
  Includes bibliographical references (p.) and index.
  Summary: Presents the life of the artist and author known primarily for his more than thirty children's books featuring Arthur the aardvark.
  ISBN 1-57765-111-1
    1. Brown, Marc Tolon--Juvenile literature. 2. Authors, American--20th century--Biography--Juvenile literature. 3. Arthur (Fictitious character : Brown)--Juvenile literature. 4. Children's stories--Authorship--Juvenile literature. [1. Brown, Marc Tolon. 2. Authors, American. 3. Illustrators.] I. Title.

PS3552.R6938 Z96 2000
813'.54--dc21
[B]   99-088856

Contents

Marc Brown

*A*s early as grammar school, Marc Brown knew he wanted to be an artist. His grandmother and uncle encouraged him. Marc also liked to tell stories.

Marc was inspired by many artists. He liked the work of Marc Chagall and Georges Seurat. He also read Maurice Sendak's *Where the Wild Things Are*. He loved the art and the story. So Marc decided to become an illustrator.

Marc attended the Cleveland Institute of Art. He studied painting. After graduation, he began to illustrate textbooks. An **editor** encouraged him to write and illustrate a book of his own. Marc wrote *Arthur's Nose*. It was published in 1976.

Since then, Marc has written and illustrated many more Arthur adventures. He has also written books with his wife, Laurene Krasny Brown. These books help children deal with problems like divorce and death.

Twenty-five years have passed since Marc created Arthur. His books have won many awards. And today, children still like to read about Arthur's long nose, his glasses, and his many friends.

Marc Brown

Early Years

*M*arc Brown was born in Erie, Pennsylvania, on November 25, 1946. His parents were LeRoy and Renita Brown. He had three sisters named Bonnie, Colleen, and Kimberly.

As a child, Marc loved to draw. His grandmother and uncle took a special interest in his art. They often gave him presents of pens, paper, and pencils.

Marc noticed his grandma saved all his drawings in a drawer. This made him feel very important. His grandma did not keep many things.

Marc's grandmother was also an imaginative storyteller. Marc learned a lot about telling stories from her. He liked to tell stories to his friends at school.

Marc also read books about artists and their paintings. He **admired** the art of Marc Chagall. When he was ten, he changed the spelling of his name from M-A-R-K to M-A-R-C. He wanted to be like Marc Chagall.

Later, Marc discovered Maurice Sendak's book *Where the Wild Things Are.* It inspired him. He saw how important art was in children's books. He wanted to draw and paint for children. After that, Marc decided he wanted to be an illustrator.

Marc's family visited the Chicago Art Institute in Illinois. Marc enjoyed the large, colorful paintings by Georges Seurat. Seeing them made him want to learn more about art.

In high school, Marc had an art teacher named Nancy Bryan. She encouraged him to try painting with watercolors. She worked closely with Marc. Soon, his painting improved.

Erie, Pennsylvania

Art School

Marc wanted to study art in college, but his parents disapproved. They wanted him to study a more practical subject. If Marc studied art, they would not pay his **tuition**.

But Marc's grandmother still supported his dream to be an artist. She gave him some money for college. In 1964, he began attending the Cleveland Institute of Art.

At the Cleveland Institute, Marc majored in painting. But he also tried printmaking, photography, **textiles**, and **graphic design**. He was still interested in illustrating. But many people at the art institute did not think book illustrations were art.

After the first year, Marc won **scholarships** to pay for his tuition. He also had part-time jobs. He worked in restaurants and he drove trucks. But he did not like those jobs.

In 1968, a television station hired Marc as an art director. Marc's new boss asked him to improve the weather report. Marc dressed the weather reporter as a fairy and used ropes to fly her onto the set. The station manager gave Marc a free Christmas ham. Then he fired Marc.

That same year, Marc married Stephanie Marini. She was a ballet dancer and a college professor. Marc graduated from the Cleveland Institute of Art in 1969. Marc and Stephanie went on to have two children, Tolon and Tucker.

The Cleveland Institute of Art

First Jobs

*A*fter graduation, Marc taught drawing at Garland Junior College in Boston. Marc also submitted some drawings to a publishing company called Houghton Mifflin.

Houghton Mifflin offered Marc work illustrating textbooks. They told Marc exactly what each drawing should look like. After awhile, Marc grew tired of this work.

Marc decided he wanted to illustrate children's **fiction**. In 1971, he illustrated his first children's book. It was called *What Makes the Sun Shine?* by Isaac Asimov.

Marc often showed his drawings to Tolon and Tucker. He listened to their ideas. Children look at pictures differently than adults. So Marc tried to think and see like a child.

What Makes the Sun Shine? was very popular. It won the Child Study Association of America's Children's Books Award for 1971.

Marc's **editor** was Emilie McLeod of the Atlantic Monthly Press. She encouraged him to write and illustrate a picture book of his own. She told him to **concentrate** on the characters and to have fun.

Isaac Asimov

The Birth of Arthur

*O*ne night, Marc's son Tolon asked to hear a bedtime story about a weird animal. Marc began to invent a tale about Arthur.

Arthur was a young **aardvark** who did not like his long nose. Tolon asked Marc to draw pictures of Arthur. He wanted to see what Arthur looked like.

Marc's first book, *Arthur's Nose*, was based on that bedtime story. It was published by Atlantic-Little Brown in 1976. After it was published, Marc stopped teaching. He wanted to have more time to write.

But at home, Marc and his wife Stephanie were not getting along. They divorced in 1977.

Marc began to write and illustrate all kinds of children's stories. Some books taught children how to count. Other books were about monsters, dogs, witches, and pickles.

Soon Marc wrote the second Arthur book, *Arthur's Eyes*. Then he started drawing the illustrations. As he drew, he noticed that Arthur's trunklike nose always hid his mouth. He could never show Arthur smiling, frowning, or speaking.

So Marc decided to draw Arthur with a shorter nose. *Arthur's Eyes* was published in 1979. Arthur's wish had come true. He had a new, short nose!

Marc and Arthur

Inventing New Stories

*M*arc wrote about many more of Arthur's experiences. He wrote *Arthur's Valentine, Arthur Goes to Camp, Arthur's Halloween*, and *Arthur's April Fool*. These became a series of books called Arthur's Adventures.

Marc also began to write a series of **rhyming** books. In 1980, he wrote *Finger Rhymes*. He went on to write *Hand Rhymes, Play Rhymes,* and *Party Rhymes*.

Then Marc took part in a study. He studied how illustrations in children's books help a child's imagination.

While working on the study, Marc met a woman named Laurene Krasny. She was a **psychologist** and a writer. Marc and Laurene were married on September 11, 1983. Soon, they had a new daughter named Eliza.

When Eliza was born, Marc wrote *Arthur's Baby*. Other Arthur stories have come from Marc's experiences, too. Marc based Grandma Thora on his own grandmother. The characters of D.W. and Francine come from the **personalities** of his three sisters. And Marc says he and Arthur are a lot alike.

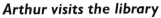

Marc writes most of his story ideas on notepaper. Then he puts them in his "idea drawer." He thinks about each story for a long time before he writes it.

Before he does any of the drawings, Marc writes the story. Then he uses pictures to add **details** to the story. Each book takes about one year to finish.

Arthur visits the library

Serious Subjects

*I*n 1984, Marc and his wife Laurene published their first book together. It was called *The Bionic Bunny Show*. It was a funny book about a superhero bunny.

Then the Browns began to write about serious subjects. When Marc's first marriage ended, he had looked for books to help him talk about divorce with his young sons. He could not find the books he needed. So in 1986, he and Laurene published *Dinosaurs Divorce*.

Together they have written more dinosaur books to help parents and children with problems. They are *Dinosaurs Travel, Dinosaurs to the Rescue, Dinosaurs Alive and Well*, and *When Dinosaurs Die*.

Marc and Laurene work as a team. Laurene works on the research and writes the text. Marc works on the illustrations. They work in separate studios. But they talk about every part of the book together.

Opposite page: Reading books about issues like divorce, death, and illness helps parents and children communicate.

Further Adventures of Arthur

Since *Arthur's Nose*, Marc has created more than 60 books featuring Arthur, his friends, and his little sister, D.W.

Arthur's Nose, Arthur's Eyes, Arthur's Valentine, The True Francine, Arthur's Halloween, Arthur Goes to Camp, and *Arthur's April Fool* were all chosen as **Children's Choice Books**. In 1980, Marc won the **Boston-Globe Horn Book Honor Award** for his illustrations in *Why the Tides Ebb and Flow*.

In 1985, *Swamp Monsters* was chosen as a Library of Congress Book of the Year. The same year, *Hand Rhymes* was chosen as a **Booklist Editor's Choice**.

In 1993, Broderbund Software made Arthur's Adventures into educational computer games. They created 12 programs that children can use to learn by playing games and making crafts with Arthur.

Arthur also has his own cartoon series. *Arthur* began on PBS in 1996. Marc helped create all the TV shows. Some **episodes** are based on the books and some are new stories. The series won **Emmy Awards** in 1997 and 1998. In 2000, PBS showed the first Arthur Christmas special. It was called "Arthur's Perfect Christmas."

A scene from "Arthur's Perfect Christmas"

Marc Brown at Home

*M*arc and his family live in Hingham, Massachusetts. His house was built in 1799. He loves to **restore** old houses. He has lived in and restored five homes.

A butcher, a cattle rancher, and a general have all owned Marc's house. It was also used as a school. Marc rebuilt it to look as it did originally.

On Martha's Vineyard, Marc also owns a small farmhouse. He and his family planted a large garden of vegetables, herbs, and berries. Marc likes to bake pies with his homegrown raspberries.

Marc collects early American art and antiques. He enjoys spending time with his family. He reads books by F. Scott Fitzgerald, Charles Dickens, and Hans Christian Anderson. He enjoys the art of Norman Rockwell, Edward Hicks, Mark Rothko, Pieter Bruegel, and Albrecht Dürer. He also likes to travel around the country each year, talking to children about Arthur.

The coast of Martha's Vineyard

Glossary

aardvark - a burrowing animal that lives south of the Sahara Desert in Africa. It eats ants and termites and is active at night.

admire - to think of with respect or approval.

Booklist Editor's Choice - a yearly award given by *Booklist* magazine. Books are chosen based on content and artistic quality, as well as special appeal to youth.

Boston-Globe Horn Book Honor Award - an award given by the *Boston Globe* and The Horn Book, Inc. for the best authors and illustrators of picture books, fiction, and nonfiction.

Children's Choice Book - an award given by the Children's Book Council and International Reading Association.

concentrate - to focus all of your attention on something.

detail - a small part.

editor - a person who makes sure a piece of writing has no errors in it before it is published.

Emmy Award - an award given out annually by the National Academy of Television Arts and Sciences to the best programs on television.

episode - one show in a continuing series of shows.

fiction - a story that is not fact.

graphic design - the art of conveying a message using type and images.

personality - the traits that make a person unique.

psychologist - a person who specializes in studying the mind and the reasons for the ways that people think and act.

restore - bring something back to its original state.

rhyme - a group of words that sound similar.

scholarship - a gift of money to help a student pay for instruction.

textiles - the art of making and using cloth.

tuition - the price or payment for instruction.

Internet Sites

Arthur's Home Page

http://www.pbs.org/wgbh/arthur

Get to know Arthur, D.W., and their friends at this site hosted by PBS. This site is also useful for teachers, librarians, and parents who want children to learn with Arthur.

Time Warner Bookmark

http://www.twbookmark.com

Search for Marc Brown at this site hosted by Time Warner, and find a biography of Marc Brown. You can also learn more about all of the books he has written.

Write to Marc Brown at:
Marc Brown
c/o Little, Brown and Company
3 Center Plaza
Boston, MA 02108

These sites are subject to change. Go to your favorite search engine and type in Marc Brown for more sites.

Index